Happiness is about being free, to become free you have to have courage to take the leap.

ENLIGHTENED PUBLISHING

© Copyright 2021-2025 - All rights reserved.
You may not reproduce, duplicate or send the contents of this book without direct written permission from the author. You cannot hereby despite any circumstance blame the publisher or hold him or her to legal responsibility for any reparation, compensations, or monetary forfeiture owing to the information included herein, either in a direct or an indirect way.
Legal Notice: This book has copyright protection. You can use the book for personal purpose. You should not sell, use, alter, distribute, quote, take excerpts or paraphrase in part or whole the material contained in this book without obtaining the permission of the author first.
Disclaimer Notice: You must take note that the information in this document is for casual reading and entertainment purposes only. We have made every attempt to provide accurate, up to date and reliable information. We do not express or imply guarantees of any kind. The persons who read admit that the writer is not occupied in giving legal, financial, medical or other advice. We put this book content by sourcing various places.
Please consult a licensed professional before you try any techniques shown in this book. By going through this document, the book lover comes to an agreement that under no situation is the author accountable for any forfeiture, direct or indirect, which they may incur because of the use of material contained in this document, including, but not limited to, —errors, omissions, or inaccuracies.

Write who you want to become, think about it and write in great detail

What risk would you take if you knew you could not fail?

What is your greatest strength? Have any of your recent actions demonstrated this strength?

What are the top five things you cherish in your life?

How old would you be if you didn't know how old you are?

When do you stop calculating risk and rewards, and just do it?

At what time in your recent past have you felt most passionate and alive?

What do you most connect with? Why?

What one piece of advice would you offer a newborn child?

Which is worse, failing or never trying?

Why do we do things we dislike and like the things we never seem to do?

What are you avoiding?

What is the one job/cause/activity that could get you out of bed happily for the rest of your life? Are you doing it now?

When it's all said and done, will you have said more than you've done?

What are you most grateful for?

What would you say is one thing you'd like to change in the world?

Do you find yourself influencing your world, or it influencing you?

Are you doing what you believe in or settling for what you're doing?

What are you committed to?

Which worries you more, doing things right or doing the right things?

If joy became the national currency, what kind of work would make you wealthy?

Have you been the kind of friend you'd want as one?

Do any of the things that used to upset you a few years ago matter at all today? What's changed?

Would you rather have less work to do or more work you enjoy doing?

What permission do you need/want to move forward?

Really, what do you have to lose if you go for it?

How different would your life be if there weren't any criticism in the world?

We're always making choices. Are you choosing for your story or for someone else's?

What if this was the last time..?

If tomorrow was my last day, would I have any regrets?

What can I do today that can shape my future in exciting ways?

What kind of impact do you want to have?

Last but not least,
live the life you want not the life others tell you or expect from you.
Society doesn't have a say in how you decide to live your life.
Be happy, make yourself happy
in order to make others, it doesn't work any other way.
There is more to life than what we see and what we were told.
It's up to us to find it!
Be happy, be you!

"Be a story worth telling!"

Know thyself. Socrates

"Keep your head clear. It doesn't matter how bright the path is if your head is always cloudy." ~Unknown

www.ingramcontent.com/pod-product-compliance
Lightning Source LLC
LaVergne TN
LVHW020426080526
838202LV00055B/5046